The POEMS of SAPPHO

A New Rendering
by

Henry De Vere Stacpoole

The Hymn To Aphrodite
Fifty-Two Fragments
Sappho To Phaon, Ovid's Heroic Epistle XV

First published 1920

First published 2020 by Aziloth Books
Copyright © 2020 Aziloth Books

All Rights Reserved. No part of this publication may be reproduced, stored in a retrieval system or transmitted in any form or by any means, electronic, mechanical, photocopying, recording, scanning or otherwise, except under the terms of the Copyright Licensing Agency Ltd, 90 Tottenham Court Road, London, W1P 0LP, UK, without the permission in writing of the Publisher. Requests to the Publisher should be via email to: info@azilothbooks.com.

Every effort has been made to contact all copyright holders. The publisher will be glad to make good in future editions any errors or omissions brought to their attention.

This publication is designed to provide authoritative and accurate information in regard to the subject matter covered. It is sold on the understanding that the Publisher is not engaged in rendering professional services.

British Library Cataloguing in Publication Data

A catalogue record for this book is available from the British Library:

ISBN–13: 978-1-911405-99-3

Illustrations

Front cover: *Sappho*, Francis Coates Jones, c. 1895.
Back cover: Map showing part of Athenian Empire c. 450 B.C., with Lesbos and the city of Mitylene labelled in red.

Title page: From *Sappho & Alcaeus*, Sir Lawrence Alma-Tadema, 1881. (Cropped from original colour painting.)

Page 28: *Death of Sappho*, Miguel Carbonell Selva, 1881.

CONTENTS

INTRODUCTION		i
FOREWORD		iv
I.	HYMN TO APHRODITE	1
II.	ODE TO ANACTORIA	2
III.	WHERE BLOOMS THE MYRTLE	2
IV.	I LOVED THEE	3
V.	INVOCATION	3
VI.	CLAÏS	4
VII.	TO A SWALLOW	4
VIII.	LOVE	5
IX.	WEDDING SONG	5
X.	EVENING	6
XI.	MAIDENHOOD	6
XII.	MOONLIGHT	7
XIII.	ORCHARD SONG	7
XIV.	DICA	8
XV.	GRACE	8
XVI.	AS ON THE HILLS	9
XVII.	TO ATTHIS	9
XVIII.	AS WIND UPON THE MOUNTAIN OAKS	10
XIX.	GOODNESS	10
XX.	THE FISHERMAN'S TOMB	11
XXI.	TIMAS	11

XXII.	DEAD SHALT THOU LIE	12
XXIII.	DEATH	12
XXIV.	ALCÆUS AND SAPPHO	13
XXV.	THE ALTAR	13
XXVI.	THE ALTAR	14
XXVII.	LOVE	14
XXVIII.	LIKE THE SWEET APPLE	15
XXIX.	PROPHESY	15
XXX.	FOR THEE	16
XXXI.	FRIEND	16
XXXII.	THE MOON HAS SET	17
XXXIII.	THE SKY	17
XXXIV.	TO HER LYRE	18
XXXV.	NEVER ON ANY MAIDEN	18
XXXVI.	* * *	19
XXXVII.	ANGER	19
XXXVIII.	ADONIS	20
XXXIX.	LEDA	20
XL.	THE CAPTIVE	21
XLI.	INVOCATION	21
XLII.	YOUTH AND AGE	22
XLIII.	FRAGMENT	22
XLIV.	THE LESBIAN SINGER	23
XLV.	ON THE TOMB OF A PRIESTES OF ARTEMIS	23
XLVI.	TO A BRIDE	24

XLVII.	HERMES	24
XLVIII.	ADONIS	25
XLIX.	SLEEP	25
L.	THY FORM IS LOVELY	26
LI.	THE BRIDEGROOM	26
LII.	REGRET	27
LIII.	FRAGMENT	27
LIV.	Ovid's SAPPHO TO PHAON	28

Sappho—a biography in brief *by Arthur S. Way, 1920*   36
(Added by Aziloth Books)

INTRODUCTION

I

Sappho lies remote from us, beyond the fashions and the ages, beyond sight, almost beyond the wing of Thought, in the world's extremest youth.

To thrill the imagination with the vast measure of time between the world of Sappho and the world of the Great War, it is quite useless to express it in years, one must express it in æons, just as astronomers, dealing with sidereal distances, think, not in miles, but in light years.

Between us and Sappho lie the Roman Empire and the age of Christ, and beyond the cross the age of Athenian culture, culminating in the white flower of the Acropolis.

Had she travelled she might have visited Nineveh before its destruction by Cyaxares, or watched the Phœnicians set sail on their African voyage at the command of Nechos. She might have spoken with Draco and Jeremiah the Prophet and the father of Gautama the founder of Buddhism. For her the Historical Past, which is the background of all thought, held little but echoes, voices, and the forms of gods, and the immediate present little but Lesbos and the Ægean Sea, whose waters had been broken by the first trireme only a hundred and fifty years before her birth.

II

Men call her the greatest lyric poet that the world has known, basing their judgment on the few perfect fragments that remain of her song. But her voice is more than the voice of a lyric poet, it is the voice of a world that has been, of a freshness and beauty that will never be again, and to give that voice a last touch of charm remains the fact that it comes to us as an echo.

For of Sappho's poetry not a single vestige remains that does not come to us reflected in the form of a quotation from the works of some admirer, some one captured by her beauty or her wisdom or the splendour of her verse, or some one, like Herodian or Apollonius the sophist of Alexandria, who takes it to exhibit the æolic use of words or accentuation, or Hephæstion, to give an example of her choriambic tetrameters.

Only one complete poem comes to us, the *Hymn to Aphrodite* quoted by Dionysius of Halicarnassus, and one almost complete, the *Ode to Anactoria*, quoted by Longinus; all other quotations are fragments: a few lines, a few words, a word, the merest traces.

What fate gave us the shipping lists of Homer, yet denied us Sappho; preserved the *Lexicon Græcum Iliadis et Odysseæ* of Apollonius, yet cut the song to Anactoria short, and reduced the song of the orchard to three lines? or decided that Sophists and Grammarians, exhibiting dry-as-dust truths, should be a medium between her and us?

Some say that her works were burned at Constantinople, or at Rome, by the Christians, and what we know of the early Christians lends colour to the statement. Some that they were burned by the Byzantine emperors and the poems of Gregory Nazianzen circulated in their place.

But whatever the fate it failed in its evil intention. Sappho remains, eternal as Sirius, and it is doubtful if her charm and her hold upon the world would have been strengthened by the full preservation of her work.

As it is, added to the longing which all great art inspires, we have the longing inspired by suggestion. That lovely figure belonging to the feet she shows us "crossed by a broidered strap of Lydian work," would it have been as beautiful unveiled as imagined? Did she long for maidenhood? Why did the swallow trouble her, and what did the daughter of Cyprus say to her in a dream?

There is not a fragment of Sappho that is not surrounded in the mind of the reader by the rainbow of suggestion. Just as the gods draped the human form to give desire imagination, so, perhaps, some god and no fate has all but hidden the mind of Sappho.

III

Looking at it in another way one might fancy that all the demons of malignity and destruction had conspired to destroy and traduce: to destroy the works and traduce the character of the poet.

The game of defamation was begun in Athens in the age of corruption by lepers, and carried on through the succeeding ages by their kind, till Welcker came with his torch and showed these gibbering ghosts standing on nothing and with nothing in their hands.

Colonel Mure tried to put Welcker's torch out, and only burned his fingers. Comparetti snuffed it, only to make it burn the brighter. But bright or dim, the torch was only intended to show the lepers. Sappho shines by her own light in the minutest fragments of her that remain—Fragments whose deathless energy, like the energy of radium, has vivified literature in all ages and times.

IV

The mind of Sappho runs through all literature like a spangled thread.

FOREWORD

Tear the red rose to pieces if you will,
The soul that is the rose you may not kill;
Destroy the page, you may, but not the words
That share eternal life with flowers and birds.

And the least words of Sappho—let them fall,
Cast where you will, some bird will rise and call,
Some flower unfold in some forsaken spot.
Hill hyacinth, or blue forget-me-not.

I

HYMN TO APHRODITE

Daughter of Zeus and Immortal,
Aphrodite, serene
Weaver of spells, at thy portal
Hear me and slay not, O Queen!

As in the past, hither to me
From thy far palace of gold,
Drawn by the doves that o'erflew me,
Come, as thou earnest of old.

Swiftly thy flock bore thee hither,
Smiling, as turned I to thee,
Spoke thou across the blue weather,
"Sappho, why callest thou me?"

"Sappho, what Beauty disdains thee,
Sappho, who wrongest thine heart,
Sappho, what evil now pains thee,
Whence sped the dart?

"Flies from thee, soon she shall follow,
Turns from thee, soon she shall love,
Seeking thee swift as the swallow,
Ingrate though now she may prove."

Come, once again to release me,
Join with my fire thy fire,
Freed from the torments that seize me,
Give me, O Queen! my desire!

II

ODE TO ANACTORIA

That man, whoever he may be,
Who sits awhile to gaze on thee,
Hearing thy lovely laugh, thy speech,
Throned with the gods he seems to me;
For when a moment to mine eyes
Thy form discloses, silently
I stand consumed with fires that rise
Like flames around a sacrifice.
Sight have I none, bells out of tune
Ring in mine ears, my tongue lies dumb;
Paler than grass in later June,
Yet daring all
   (To thee I come).

III

WHERE BLOOMS THE MYRTLE

O Muse, upon thy golden throne,
Far in the azure, fair, alone.
Sing what the Teian sweetly sang,—
The Teian sage whose lineage sprang
Where blooms the myrtle in the gay
Land of fair women far away.

IV

I LOVED THEE

> I loved thee, Atthis, once,
> once long ago.

V

INVOCATION

> Goddess of Cyprus come (where beauty lights
> The way) and serve in cups of gold these lips
> With nectar, mixed by love with all delights
> Of golden days, and dusk of amorous nights.

VI

CLAÏS

> I have a daughter,
> Claïs fair,
> Poised like a golden flower in air,
> Lydian treasures her limbs outshine
> (Claïs, beloved one,
> Claïs mine!)

VII

TO A SWALLOW

> Pandion's daughter—O fair swallow,
> Why dost thou weary me—
>   (Where should I follow?)

VIII

LOVE

Sweet mother, at the idle loom I lean,
Weary with longing for the boy that still
Remains a dream of loveliness—to fill
My soul, my life, at Aphrodite's will.

IX

WEDDING SONG

Workmen lift high
The beams of the roof,
Hymenæus!

Like Ares from sky
Comes the groom to the bride.
Hymenæus!

Than men who must die
Stands he taller in pride,
Hymenæus!

X

EVENING

> Children astray to their mothers, and goats to the herd,
> Sheep to the shepherd, through twilight the wings of the bird,
> All things that morning has scattered with fingers of gold,
> All things thou bringest, O Evening! at last to the fold.

XI

MAIDENHOOD

> Maidenhood! Maidenhood! where hast thou gone from me.
> Whither, O Slain!
>
> I shall return to thee, I who have gone from thee, never again.

XII

MOONLIGHT

> The stars around the fair moon fade
> Against the night,
> When gazing full she fills the glade
> And spreads the seas with silvery light.

XIII

ORCHARD SONG

> Cool murmur of water through apple-wood
> Troughs without number
> The whole orchard fills, whilst the leaves
> Lend their music to slumber.

XIV

DICA

With flowers fair adorn thy lustrous hair,
Dica, amidst thy locks sweet blossoms twine,
With thy soft hands, for so a maiden stands
Accepted of the gods, whose eyes divine
Are turned away from her—though fair as May
She waits, but round whose locks no flowers shine.

XV

GRACE

What country maiden charms thy heart,
However fair, however sweet,
Who has not learned by gracious Art
To draw her dress around her feet?

XVI

AS ON THE HILLS

> As on the hills the shepherds trample the hyacinth
>   down,
> Staining the earth with darkness, there where a
>   flower has blown.

XVII

TO ATTHIS

> Hateful my face is to thee,
> Hateful to thee beyond speaking,
> Atthis, who fliest from me
> Like a white bird Andromeda seeking.

XVIII

AS WIND UPON THE MOUNTAIN OAKS

As wind upon the mountain oaks in storm,
So Eros shakes my soul, my life, my form.

XIX

GOODNESS

He who is fair is good to look upon;
He who is good is fair, though youth be gone.

XX

THE FISHERMAN'S TOMB

> Over the fisher Pelagon Meniscus his father set
> The oar worn by the wave, the trap, and the fishing net;—
> For all men, and for ever, memorials there to be
> Of the luckless life of the fisher, the labourer of the sea.

XXI

TIMAS

> This is the dust of Timas, who, unwed,
> Passed hence to Proserpina's house of gloom.
> In mourning all her sorrowing playmates shed
> Their curls and cast the tribute on her tomb.

XXII

DEAD SHALT THOU LIE

    Dead shalt thou lie for ever, and forgotten,
    For whom the flowers of song have never bloomed;
    A wanderer amidst the unbegotten,
    In Hades' house a shadow ay entombed.

XXIII

DEATH

    Death is an evil, for the gods choose breath;
    Had Death been good the gods had chosen Death.

XXIV

ALCÆUS AND SAPPHO

ALCÆUS

Sweet violet-weaving Sappho, whose soft smile
My tongue should free,
Lo, I would speak, but shame holds me the while
I gaze on thee.

SAPPHO

Hadst thou but felt desire of noble things,
Hadst not thy tongue proposed to speak no good,
Thy words had not been destitute of wings,
Nor shame thine eyes subdued.

XXV

THE ALTAR

Then the full globed moon arose, and there
The women stood as round an altar fair.

XXVI

THE ALTAR

> And thus at times, in Crete, the women there
> Circle in dance around the altar fair;
> In measured movement, treading as they pass
> With tender feet the soft bloom of the grass.

XXVII

LOVE

> All delicacy unto me is lovely, and for me,
> O Love!
> Thy wings are as the midday fire,
> Thy splendour as the sun above.

XXVIII

LIKE THE SWEET APPLE

> Like the sweet apple that reddens
> At end of the bough—
> Far end of the bough—
> Left by the gatherer's swaying,
> Forgotten, so thou.
> Nay, not forgotten, ungotten,
> Ungathered (till now).

XXIX

PROPHESY

> Methinks hereafter in some later spring
> Echo will bear to men the songs we sing.

XXX

FOR THEE

    For thee, unto the altar will I lead
    A white goat—
        To the altar by the sea;
    And there, where waves advance and waves recede,
    A full libation will I pour for thee.

XXXI

FRIEND

    Friend, face me so and raise
    Unto my face thy face,
    Unto mine eyes thy gaze,
    Unto my soul its grace.

XXXII

THE MOON HAS SET

> The moon has set beyond the seas,
> And vanished are the Pleiades;
> Half the long weary night has gone,
> Time passes—yet I lie alone.

XXXIII

THE SKY

> I think not with these two
> White arms to touch the blue.

XXXIV

TO HER LYRE

> Singing, O shell, divine!
> Let now thy voice be mine.

XXXV

NEVER ON ANY MAIDEN

> Never on any maiden, the golden sun shall shine,
> Never on any maiden whose wisdom matches thine.

XXXVI

I spoke with Aphrodite in a dream.

XXXVII

ANGER

When anger stirs thy breast,
Speak not at all
(For words, once spoken, rest
Beyond recall).

XXXVIII

ADONIS

>Ah for Adonis!
>(Where the willows sigh
>The call still comes
>Through spring's sweet mystery.)

XXXIX

LEDA

>They say, 'neath leaf and blossom
>Leda found in the gloom
>An egg, white as her bosom,
>Under an iris bloom.

XL

THE CAPTIVE

> Now Love has bound me, trembling, hands and feet,
> O Love so fatal, Love so bitter-sweet.

XLI

INVOCATION

> Come to me, O ye graces,
> Delicate, tender, fair;
> Come from your heavenly places,
> Muses with golden hair.

XLII

YOUTH AND AGE

If love thou hast for me, not hate,
Arise and find a younger mate;
For I no longer will abide
Where youth and age lie side by side.

XLIII

FRAGMENT

From heaven returning;
Red of hue, his chlamys burning
Against the blue.

XLIV

THE LESBIAN SINGER

>Upstanding, as the Lesbian singer stands
>Above the singers of all other lands.

XLV

ON THE TOMB OF A PRIESTESS OF ARTEMIS

>Voiceless I speak, and from the tomb reply
>Unto Æthopia, Leto's child, was I
>Vowed by the daughter of Hermocleides,
>Who was the son of Saonaïades.
>O virgin queen, unto my prayer incline,
>Bless him and cast thy blessing on our line.

XLVI

TO A BRIDE

> Bride, around whom the rosy loves are flying,
> Sweet image of the Cyprian undying,
> The bed awaits thee; go, and with him lying,
> Give to the groom thy sweetness, softly sighing.
> May Hesperus in gladness pass before thee,
> And Hera of the silver throne bend o'er thee.

XLVII

HERMES

> Ambrosia there was mixed, and from his station
> Hermes the bowl for waiting gods outpoured;
> Then raised they all their cups and made oblation,
> Blessing the bridegroom (by the bride adored).

XLVIII

ADONIS

> Tender Adonis stricken is lying.
> What, Cytherea, now can we do?
> Beat your breasts, maidens, Adonis is dying,
> Rending your garments (the white fragments strew).

XLIX

SLEEP

> With eyes of darkness,
> The sleep of night.

L

THY FORM IS LOVELY

>Thy form is lovely and thine eyes are honeyed,
>>O'er thy face the pale
>Clear light of love lies like a veil.
>Bidding thee rise,
>With outstretched hands,
>Before thee Aphrodite stands.

LI

THE BRIDEGROOM

>Joy born of marriage thou provest,
>Bridegroom thrice blest,
>Holding the maiden thou lovest
>Clasped to thy breast.

LII

REGRET

    Those unto whom I have given,
    These have my heart most riven.

LIII

FRAGMENT

    Upon thy girl friend's white and tender breast,
    Sleep thou, and on her bosom find thy rest.

SAPPHO to PHAON

A new rendering of Ovid's Heroic Epistle, XV.

LIV

SAPPHO TO PHAON

A new rendering of Ovid's Heroic Epistle, XV.

I

Phaon, most lovely, closest to my heart,
Can your dear eyes forget, or must I stand
Confessed in name, beloved that thou art,
Lost to my touch and in another land.
Sappho now calls thee, lyre and Lyric Muse
    Forgotten, and the tears born of her wrongs
Blinding her eyes, upturned but to refuse
Phœbus, the fountain of all joyous songs.

I burn, as when in swiftness, past the byres,
Flame takes the corn, borne by the winds that blow;
For what are Ætna's flames to my desires,
Thou, who by Ætna wanderest, O Thou!
The Lyric Muse has turned, as I from her,
Peace, Peace alone can join us once again,
The blue sea in its solitude lies fair,
But, desolate, I turn from it in pain.
No more the girls of Lesbos move my heart,
My blameless love for them is now no more,
Before my love for thee all loves depart,
Cold wanderer thou upon a distant shore.

O thou art lovely! wert thou garbed like him,
Apollo by thy side a shade would be.
Garland thy tresses with the ivy dim
And Bacchus would be less himself, by thee.
Apollo, yet, who bent, as Bacchus fell,
One to the Cretan, one to Daphne's fire,
Beside me, what are they? I cast my spell
O'er seas and lands, the music of my lyre

Echoes across the world where mortals dwell,
Renders the earth in tune with my desire.

Alcæus strikes Olympus with his song,
Boldly and wild his music finds its star.
Unto the human does my voice belong
And Aphrodite smiles on me from far.
Have I no charms? has genius lost her touch
To turn simplicity to beauty's zone?
Am I so small, whose towering height is such
That in the world of men I stand alone?

Yea, I am brown—an Æthiopian's face
Turned Perseus from his path, a flame of fire.
White doves or dark, which hath the finer grace?
Are they not equal, netted by desire?

If by no charm except thine own sweet charm
Thou can'st be moved, ah then, alas, for me!
Fires of the earth thy coldness will not warm,
And Phaon's self must Phaon's lover be.

Yet once, ah once! forgetful of the world,
You lay engirdled by this world of mine,
Those nights remain, be earth to darkness hurled,
Deathless, as passion's ecstasy divine.
My songs around you were the only birds,
My voice the only music, in your fire
With kisses, burning yet, you killed my words
And found my kisses sweeter than desire.
I filled you with delight, when close embraced;
In the last act of love I gave you heaven,
And yet again, delirious as we faced,
And yet again, till in exhaustion, even
Love's self half died and nothing more remained,
But earth and life half lost, and heaven gained.

And now, Sicilian girls—O heart of mine,
Why was I born so far from Sicily?—
Sicilian girls, unto my words incline,
Beware of smiles, of insincerity,
Beware the words that once belonged to me,
The fruits of passion and the seeds of grief;
O Cyprian by the fair Sicilian sea,
Sappho now calls thee, turn to her relief!

Shall Fortune still pursue me, luckless one,
With hounds of woe pursue me down the years?
Sorrow was mine since first I saw the sun,
The ashes of my parents knew my tears.
My brother cast the gifts of life away
For one unworthy of all gifts but gold,
Grief follows grief and on this woeful day
An infant daughter in my arms I hold.

Fates! What more can ye do, what more essay?
Phaon! ah yes, he is the last, I know.
The first, the all, the grave that once was gay,
The dark veil o'er my purple robe ye throw,
My curls no more are curls, nor scent the air
With perfume from the flowers Egyptians grow,
The gold that bound these locks of mine so fair
Has parted for the wind these locks to blow.
All arts of love were mine when he was by,
Whose sun is now the sun of Sicily.

Phaon! when I was born, the mystic three
Called Aphrodite on my birth to gaze,
And then the Cyprian, turning, called on thee
To be my fate and fill my dreams and days.
Thou for whose sake Aurora's eyes might turn
From Cephalus, or Cynthia give thee sleep,
Pouring oblivion from night's marble urn,
Bidding Endymion to watch thy sheep!

—Lo! as I write I weep, and nought appears
But Love, half veiled by broken words and tears.

You! you! who left me without kiss or tear
Or word, to murmur softly like a child
Begotten of thy voice, deception were
Less cruel far than silence, you who smiled
Falsely so often, had you no false phrase—
You who so often had false tales to tell—
No voice there, at the parting of our ways,
To say "Farewell, O Love!" or just "Farewell"!

I had no gift to give you when you passed,
And wrongs were all the gifts received from thee,
I had no words to tell you at the last
But these: "Forgo not life, forget not me."
And when I heard, told by some casual tongue,
That thou wert gone, Grief turned me then to stone,
Voiceless I stood as though I ne'er had sung,
Pulseless and lost, for ever more alone.
Without a sigh, without a tear to shed,
Grief held me, Grief who has no word to say.

Then, rising as one rises from the dead,
My soul broke forth as one breaks forth to slay.
Rending and wounding all this frame of mine,
Cursing the Gods, the moments and the years,
Now like the clouds of storm, where lightnings shine,
Uplifted, then resolving into tears.
Debased, when turns my brother in his scorn
My grief to laughter, pointing to my child;
Till madness takes me as the fire the corn
And, in reviling thee, I stand reviled.
Ah! but at night, At night I turn to thee.
In dreams our limbs are joined, as flame with flame,
In dreams again your arms are girdling me,
I taste your soul in joys I blush to name.

Ah! but the day that follows on the night,
The emptiness that drives me to the plain
To seek those spots that knew my lost delight,
The grotto that shall shield us not again.

Here lies the grass we pressed in deeds of love,
Lips, limbs entwined — I kiss the ground today.
The herbs lie withered, and the birds that move
Are songless, and the very trees are grey.
Night takes the day and falls upon the groves,
The nightingale alone is left to cry,
Lamenting, in the song that sorrow loves,
To Tereus she calls, to Phaon, I.

II

There is a spring, through whose cool water shows
The sand like silver, clear as seen through air.
There is a spring, above whose mirror grows
A lotus like a grove in flower fair.
Here, as I lay in tears, a spirit stood
Born of the water, then she called to me,
Sappho, pursuing Love, by Grief pursued,
Sappho, beside the blue Leucadian sea
There stands a rock, and there above the caves,
Whose wandering echoes reach Apollo's fane,
Down leaping to the blue and breaking waves,
Lovers find sleep, nor dream of love again.
Deucalion here found ease from Pyrrah's scorn,
Sappho arise, and where the sharp cliffs fall,
Thy body, that had better not been born,
Cast to the waves, the blue, blue waves that call.
I rise, and weeping silently, I go.
My fear is great, my love is greater still.

Better oblivion than the love I know,
Kinder than Phaon's is the blue wave's will.

Ye favouring breezes, guard me on this day,
Love, lend your pinions, waft me o'er the sea
Where, lovely Phœbus, on thy shrine I'll lay
My lyre, with this inscription unto thee:
"Sappho to Phœbus consecrates her lyre,
Unto the God the gift, the fire to fire."

III

Alas! and woe is me.
        But must I go?
O Phaon, Phœbus' self to me is less
Than Phaon—will you cast me down below
All broken, for the cruel rocks to press
This breast, that loved thee, ruined?—Ah! the song
Born of the Muses leaves me and the lyre
Is voiceless—they no more to me belong,
And in this darkness dies the heavenly fire.

Farewell, ye girls of Lesbos, fare ye well;
No more the groves shall answer to my song,
No more these hands shall wake the lyre to tell
Of Love, of Life—to Phaon they belong,
And he has fled.
        O Loveliness, return,
Make once again my soul to sing in joy,
Feed once again this heart with fires that burn,
Gods! can no prayers avail but to destroy,
No songs bring back the lost, no sighs recall
The lost that was my love, my life, my all?

Return! Return!
    Raise to the wind thy sail,
Across the sea bring back to me the years,
Eros shall lend to thee the favouring gale,
The track is sure where Aphrodite steers.
Let thy white sail be lifted on the rim
Of sky that marks the dark dividing seas.
Failing that far-off sail, remain the dim
Blue depths where once Deucalion found release.
Failing that far-off sail, the waves shall give
Death, or Forgetfulness, whilst still I live.

THE END

SAPPHO—a biography in brief

Below is the Introduction from Arthur S. Way's *Sappho and the Vigil of Venus*, 1920, which gives a useful account of Sappho's provenance and the esteem with which her works were regarded.
Aziloth Books

The fame of Sappho, as the greatest poetess of all time, rests mainly on tradition, which for us moderns is confirmed by one complete poem, two incomplete ones, and over 170 fragments, one consisting of six lines, ten of four, seven of three, twenty-seven of two, and the rest of not more than one line, sometimes of only one word. No other poet inherits such great fame on so slight a foundation. Yet none is, by universal consent, more incontestably pre-eminent in his sphere.

It is remarkable that, were it not for quotations by writers on style, grammarians and lexicographers, not a line of hers would have survived to our times. Yet her poems were still extant till well on in the Christian Era. They seem, from accounts which have come down to us, to have been systematically hunted out and destroyed in an outburst of fanatical religious zeal kindled by medieval ecclesiastics. Scaliger even places their destruction as late as 1073 A.D., when bonfires were made at Rome and Constantinople of the poems of Sappho and other "heathen singers," under Pope Gregory VII. Hence the men of old who were so unanimous in praise of her were writing for readers who could perfectly estimate the value of their opinion; and we find no evidence that it was ever challenged. As Homer was called *par excellence* "*the* Poet," so Sappho was styled "*the* Poetess." Plato gives her a place among the intellectual giants whom he names "the Wise." Plutarch says the recital of her poems cast a spell of enchantment over an audience, and adds that while he read them, to touch the wine-cup seemed a profanation. Writers in the Greek

Anthology acclaim her as The Tenth Muse, Daughter of Eros and Aphrodite, the Pride of Hellas, the Companion of Apollo, the Flower of the Graces. Aristotle says that the Lesbians so gloried in her, that " woman as she was," they stamped her image on their coins, just as other peoples set the heads of gods and goddesses on theirs. Dionysius of Halicarnassus, the famous writer on literary style, quotes a poem of hers (the *Hymn to Aphrodite*) as an example of absolute perfection in technique, in mastery of the music of verse: "the language," he says, "ripples softly and smoothly along, the words seem to nestle together, to be interwoven by natural affinities."

Longinus, in his *Treatise on the Sublime* quotes the Second Ode in this collection[1] as an amazing revelation of the interaction of the soul and the mortal frame under love's overwhelming passion. Strabo, who lived in the time of Augustus and Tiberius, in his *Geography*, says of the island of Lesbos: "Here flourished Sappho, who was something wonderful; never within the memory of man has any woman been known who could in the least degree be compared to her for poetic genius."

It seems almost superfluous to quote the opinions of modem poets and critics, who possess but a few gems out of a vast treasure-hoard. How great it was we may infer from the record that nine books of her lyric odes were known to the ancients, that she was the chief acknowledged writer of Epithalamia, or Marriage Songs, that her Hymns of Invocation to various deities are mentioned with special praise, and that she wrote many epigrams and elegies.

The manuscript in which the recently discovered *Ode to Anactoria*[2] was found bears the tantalizing title *The First Book of the Lyrics of Sappho, 1,332 lines*—of which but fragments remain! Yet from the long roll of great names we will venture to quote three of our writers who have testified to her glory. Addison wrote: "Her

---

[1] Arthur S. Day's collection, the Second Ode being *To a Beloved One*.   *ed., Aziloth Books*

[2] II, p. 2 of Stacpoole's collection.   *ed., Aziloth Books*

soul seems to have been made up of love and poetry . . . her works are filled with bewitching tenderness and rapture." J. Addington Symonds says: "The world has suffered no greater literary loss than the loss of Sappho's poems. So perfect are the smallest fragments preserved that we muse in a sad rapture of astonishment to think what the complete poems must have been. Of all the poets of the world, of all the illustrious artists of all literature, Sappho is the one whose every word has a peculiar and unmistakable perfume, a seal of absolute perfection and illimitable grace." Swinburne confessed that he despaired of adequately translating her. Of his attempt at an expanded paraphrase (in "Anactoria") of some fragments of her poems, he exclaimed "No one can feel more deeply than I do the inadequacy of my work. It is as near as I can come ; and no man can come close to her . . . her verses seem akin to fire and air, being themselves 'air and fire'; other element there is none in them."

Sappho was a native of the island of Lesbos: she lived towards the close of the seventh and early part of the sixth centuries B.C. She was contemporaneous with, in Hebrew history, the days just preceding the Babylonian Captivity; in Greek history, the time of Solon; in Roman history, the first of the Tarquins. Her father died when she was a child; her mother, whose name was Kleïs, may have survived to the days of her fame. She had two brothers, of whom Larichus was public cupbearer of the city of Mitylene, and, as this office could only be held by high-born youths, it follows that Sappho's family belonged to the aristocracy. Her second brother, Charaxus, has a romantic history. He sailed to Egypt, his merchandise being the celebrated Lesbian wine, and there saw a girl of surpassing loveliness, who, having been probably kidnapped by pirates, had been sold into slavery. He ransomed her at a heavy price, and made her, the world-famed Rhodopis (or Doriche, as Sappho names her in a poem), his wife, though afterwards it was said that she made merchandise of her beauty, and became very wealthy. Some Greek writers asserted that it was she who built one of the pyramids, herein confusing her with another Rhodopis, a name given to the Egyptian queen Nitocris, of whom the "golden slipper" story was told, which has survived in our nursery-legend of Cinderella. Unhappily, the poetess excited her brother's resentment by her objection to his connection with this frail beauty, and found it no easy task to appease him.[1]

If we are to conclude that all her poems in which she speaks in the first person express her own personal experience—a theory which would land us in some queer conclusions if we applied it, say, to Burns—not only was Sappho's mother living in the days of her fame, but she had a daughter named after her mother, Kleïs, a very fair, sweet and dear maiden.

The beauty of the women of Lesbos was early sung by Homer, and Sappho was dowered with no small share of it. A poet in the Greek Anthology sings how her starry eyes reflected her genius, and compares the beauty of her face to that of Aphrodite. As to Alcaeus the poet's love for her, and her love for Phaon, and her despairing leap from the Leucadian Rock to a death in the sea, because that love was unrequited—these stories are rejected by the learned as the inventions of later romancers.

The Aeolian ladies of Lesbos were like those of the court of our Queen Elizabeth, intellectual and cultured. They formed clubs among themselves for the cultivation of poetry and music; and the most famous of these aesthetic coteries gathered round Sappho.

Readers who know something of the passionate attachments between girls at school and college, of their adoration for each other and their teachers, will not think it strange that we find evidence in these poems of similar links of love between Sappho and some of her girl-students, that we find records of rapturous happiness, of adoring worship, of burning reproaches, passioning and thrilling through these immortal lines. Human nature has not changed in five-and-twenty centuries. Disraeli, in *Coningsby*, wrote: "At school,

---

[1] Among recent discoveries in Egypt is a fragment containing one of her attempts at reconciliation.

friendship is a passion. It entrances the being; it tears the soul. All loves of after life can never bring its rapture or its wretchedness; no bliss so absorbing, no pangs of jealousy or despair so crushing and so keen! What tenderness and what devotion; what illimitable confidence; infinite revelations of inmost thoughts; what ecstatic present and romantic future; what bitter estrangements and what melting reconciliations; what scenes of wild recrimination, agitating explanations, passionate correspondence; what insane sensitiveness, and what frantic sensibility; what earthquakes of the heart and whirlwinds of the soul are confined in that simple phrase—a school-friendship!" Those words might have been penned by one who had been listening to the echoes that have pealed down the corridors of time from those halls where gathered the girl-friends of Sappho.

But in after-ages, when nameless vices became rife in Greece, and when the days of intellectual queens at Lesbos were no more, and the degraded daughters of that island had won an evil pre-eminence of wantonness; then coarse-minded comic writers, for whom pure love between persons of the same sex—as of David and Jonathan, Achilles and Patroclus, Tennyson and Arthur Hallam—was inconceivable, attributed their own foul imaginings to those fair and sweet women of a golden age. They cast the filth gendered in their own souls upon the robes of Sappho—these wallowers in foulness who thought that they could defile the stars with bespatterings from their sties!

Arthur Sanders Way, 1920

AZILOTH BOOKS

Aziloth Books publishes a wide range of titles ranging from hard-to-find esoteric books – *Parchment Books* – to classic works on fiction, politics and philosophy – *Cathedral Classics*. Our newest venture is *Aziloth Books Children's Classics*, with vibrant new covers and illustrations to complement some of the world's very best children's tales. All our imprints are offered to the reader at a competitive price and through as many mediums and outlets as possible.

We are committed to excellent book production and strive, whenever possible, to add value to our titles with original images, maps and author introductions. With the premium on space in most modern dwellings, we also endeavour – within the limits of good book design – to make our products as slender as possible, allowing more books to be fitted into a given bookshelf area.

We are a small, approachable company and would love to hear any of your comments and suggestions on our plans, products, or indeed on absolutely anything.

Aziloth Books, Rimey Law, Rookhope, Co. Durham, DL13 2BL, England.
t: 01388-517600 e: info@azilothbooks.com w: www.azilothbooks.com

Cathedral Classics hosts an array of classic literature, from erudite ancient tomes to avant-garde, twentieth-century masterpieces, all of which deserve a place in your home. All the world's great novelists are here, Jane Austen, Dickens, Conrad, Arthur Machen and Henry James, brushing shoulders with such disparate luminaries as Sun Tzu, Marcus Aurelius, Kipling, Friedrich Nietzsche, Machiavelli, and Omar Khayam. A small selection is detailed below:

Herland	Charlotte Perkins Gilman
The Rubaiyat of Omar Khayyam	Omar Khayyam
The Sign of the Four	Arthur Conan Doyle
The Picture of Dorian Gray	Oscar Wilde
Flatland	Edwin A. Abbott
The Coming Race	Edward Bulwer-Lytton
Beyond Good and Evil	Friedrich Nietzsche
The Genealogy of Morals	Friedrich Nietzsche
England, My England	D. H. Lawrence
The Castle of Otranto	Horace Walpole
Self-Reliance, & Other Essays (series1&2)	Ralph W. Emmerson
The Art of War	Sun Tzu
A Shepherd's Life	W. H. Hudson
To the Lighthouse; Mrs. Dalloway	Virginia Woolf
The Sorrows of Young Werther	Johann W. Goethe
Demian: the story of a youth	Herman Hesse
Analects	Confucius
The Subjection of Women	John Stuart Mill
Rights of Man	Thomas Paine
Progress and Poverty	Henry George
Captains Courageous	Rudyard Kipling
The Meditations of Marcus Aurelius	Marcus Aurelius
The Social Contract	Jean Jacques Rousseau
War is a Racket	Smedley D. Butler
The Dead	James Joyce
The Autobiography of Benjamin Franklin	Benjamin Franklin
Frankenstein or the Modern Prometheus	Mary Shelley
Anarchy	Errico Malatesta
The Interesting Narrative...Olaudah Equiano...	Olaudah Equiano
The History of Mary Prince, a West Indian slave	Mary Prince
The Strange Case of Dr. Jekyll & Mr. Hyde: Illus...	Robert Louis Stevenson
Imperialism, the Highest Stage of Capitalism...	Vladimir Lenin
The Prince: Translated by N. H. Thompson with...	Niccolo Machiavelli
The Witch Cult in Western Europe: the Original Text...	Margaret Murray
Bankers and Other Rogues: A Brief History...	Alexander Del Mar

Obtainable at all good online and local bookstores.
View Aziloth Books' full list at: www.azilothbooks.com

Parchment Books enshrines the concept of the oneness of all true religious traditions – that "the light shines from many different lanterns". Our list below offers titles from both eastern and western spiritual traditions, including Christian, Judaic, Islamic, Daoist, Hindu and Buddhist mystical texts, as well as books on alchemy, hermeticism, paganism, etc..

By bringing together such spiritual texts, we hope to make esoteric and occult knowledge more readily available to those ready to receive it. We do not publish grimoires or any titles pertaining to the left hand path. Titles include:

The Prophet	Khalil Gibran
The Madman: His Parables and Poems	Khalil Gibran
Abandonment to Divine Providence	Jean-Pierre de Caussade
Corpus Hermeticum	G. R. S. Mead (trans.)
The Holy Rule of St Benedict	St. Benedict of Nursia
An Outline of Occult Science	Rudolf Steiner
The Dialogue Of St Catherine Of Siena	St. Catherine of Siena
Esoteric Christianity	Annie Besant
Thought-Forms*	Annie Besant
The Teachings of Zoroaster	Shapurji A. Kapadia
Dweller on Two Planets	Phylos the Thibetan
The Imitation of Christ	Thomas à Kempis
The Interior Castle	St. Teresa of Avila
Songs of Innocence & Experience*	William Blake
The Secret of the Rosary	St. Louis Marie de Montfort
Kundalini – an occult experience	George S. Arundale
The Kingdom of God is Within You	Leo Tolstoy
A Textbook of Theosophy	Charles W. Leadbetter
Chuang Tzu: Daoist Teachings	Chuang Tzu
Practical Mysticism	Evelyn Underhill
Tao Te Ching (Lao Tzu's Book of the Way)	Tzu, Lao
Tertium Organum	P. D. Ouspensky
The Kebra Negast	E. A. Wallis Budge
Esoteric Buddhism	Alfred Percy Sinnett
The Machinery of the Mind	Dion Fortune
The Kybalion & The Emerald Tablet of Hermes	Three Initiates
The Psychology of Man's Possible Evolution	Peter D. Ouspensky
Christianity as Mystical Fact and the Mysteries of ...	Rudolf Steiner
The Story of a Soul: The Autobiography of...	Saint Thérèse
The Confessions of Saint Augustine: An Intimate...	Saint Augustine
The Dhammapada: The Buddha's "Way of ...	Buddha
Religion Medici: The Religion of a Physician	Thomas Browne

* With colour illustrations

Obtainable at all good online and local bookstores.
View Aziloth Books' full list at: www.azilothbooks.com

AZILOTH BOOKS — Children's Classics

Aziloth Books is passionate about bringing the very best in children's classics fiction to the next generation of book-lovers. We believe in the transforming power of children's books to encourage a life-long love of reading, and publish only the best authors and illustrators. With its original design and outstanding quality, our highly successful list has something to suit every age and interest. Titles include:

The Railway Children	Edith Nesbit
Anne of Green Gables	LucyMaud Montgomery
What Katy Did	Susan Coolidge
Puck of Pook's Hill	Rudyard Kipling
The Jungle Books	Rudyard Kipling
Just So Stories	Rudyard Kipling
Alice Through the Looking Glass	Charles Dodgson
Alice's Adventures in Wonderland*	Charles Dodgson
Black Beauty	Anna Sewell
The War of the Worlds	H. G Wells
The Time Machine	H. G .Wells
The Sleeper Awakes	H. G. Wells
The Invisible Man	H. G. Wells
The Lost World	Sir Arthur Conan Doyle
Gulliver's Travels*	Jonathan Swift
Catriona (David Balfour)	Robert Louis Stevenson
The Water Babies	Charles Kingsley
The First Men in the Moon	Jules Verne
The Secret Garden	Frances Hodgson Burnett
A Little Princess	Frances Hodgson Burnett
Peter Pan*	J. M. Barrie
The Song of Hiawatha*	Henry W. Longfellow
Tales from Shakespeare	Charles and Mary Lamb
The Story of My Life (with photo album)	Helen Keller
The Wonderful Wizard of Oz	L. Frank Baum

*Illustrations in colour

Obtainable at all good online and local bookstores.
View Aziloth Books' full list at: www.azilothbooks.com

www.ingramcontent.com/pod-product-compliance
Lightning Source LLC
Chambersburg PA
CBHW061258040426
42444CB00010B/2418